BIG RED

With love, to Kerry
C. S.

To Possum, for support and
warm fur, and to Gordon, for
the big question and courage
G. B.

Text copyright © 2013 by Claire Saxby
Illustrations copyright © 2013 by Graham Byrne

First U.S. edition 2015

Library of Congress Catalog Card
Number 2013955949
ISBN 978-0-7636-7075-7

SCP 19 18 17 16 15 14
10 9 8 7 6 5 4 3 2 1

Printed in Humen, Dongguan, China

This book was typeset in Journal.
The illustrations were created with
charcoal and digital media.

Candlewick Press
99 Dover Street
Somerville, Massachusetts 02144

visit us at www.candlewick.com

KANGAROO

CLAIRE SAXBY illustrated by **GRAHAM BYRNE**

CANDLEWICK PRESS

In the center of Australia,
far inland, where ocean
is a dim memory, the sun
floats on the waves of
another bake-earth day.
In the long shadows, a
big red kangaroo licks
his forearms and lets
the early evening breeze
wash over him.

Red Kangaroo appears relaxed, almost lazy. But if you watch closely, you'll see his ears twitch. He is alert. Around him, females, joeys, and younger male kangaroos also stir. This is his mob.

Red kangaroos live in families called mobs.
The group size varies, but usually contains
a dominant male, at least one female, and
several joeys (baby kangaroos).

The heat eases with the approaching nightfall. It is breakfast time for Red's mob. Around them, the night orchestra begins. Red rises and leads his mob beyond the shadow line in search of grasses.

Red kangaroos are most active at dusk and dawn, although they will graze throughout the night.
The grasses they eat are difficult to digest. When they rest, they sometimes regurgitate their food and chew it again.

A sudden storm rinses the air
and sweeps dust into mud rivulets.
Red flattens his body, extends his
tail, and bounds toward the trees,
his mob close behind.

A kangaroo's tail is long and strong. It aids in balance, almost like another leg. When a kangaroo moves at full speed, its tail acts like a rudder.

Other groups of kangaroos join them in the shelter of the trees. Red watches.

A young male wanders too close to Red's mob. Red stands proud, shoulders back. It is a warning. The young kangaroo hops away. He is no threat today.

Each mob has a single strong male as its leader. If he shows signs of weakness, other males will challenge his position to become the head of the mob. A full-grown male red kangaroo can weigh as much as 200 pounds (90 kilograms) and may reach 6 feet (1.8 meters) in height when standing.

The rain ends as suddenly as it began, and the kangaroos venture out again.

Rainwater loiters in shallow pools, and Red drinks. The mob is joined by wallaroos, thorny devils, and a spinifex hopping mouse. There is not much water here in the middle of the land, in the middle of the dry season.

A wallaroo is a small marsupial,
and a thorny devil is a lizard with thick spurs over its skin.
Spinifex is a spiky grass that grows in clumps.
Kangaroos get most of their water from the plants they eat, but
they will drink from puddles and streams if they can. When the season
is good and food is plentiful, they may not drink much water at all.

Red cannot relax while other males
are so close. It is time to move. He sets
off east, his mob close behind. His hops
are long. Each landing pushes air from
his lungs; each bound fills them.

When red kangaroos want to travel faster, they make each hop longer rather than taking more hops. This conserves their energy so they can travel long distances.

Red halts at a broad, shallow plain that sits lower
than the surrounding land. This depression caught
a shower last week and now blushes green in the
moonlight. Red sniffs the air, listens, then settles to eat.
Tuft by green tuft, he chews and swallows.
The night is alive with stars. Animals too. Most of
them Red can ignore. Only the dingo is dangerous,
with his stealth and sharp teeth.

Red kangaroos have few natural predators. Large lizards called goannas sometimes take joeys in the daytime. When the earth cools, goannas move more slowly. Then it is night-hunting dogs, known as dingoes, that are more dangerous.

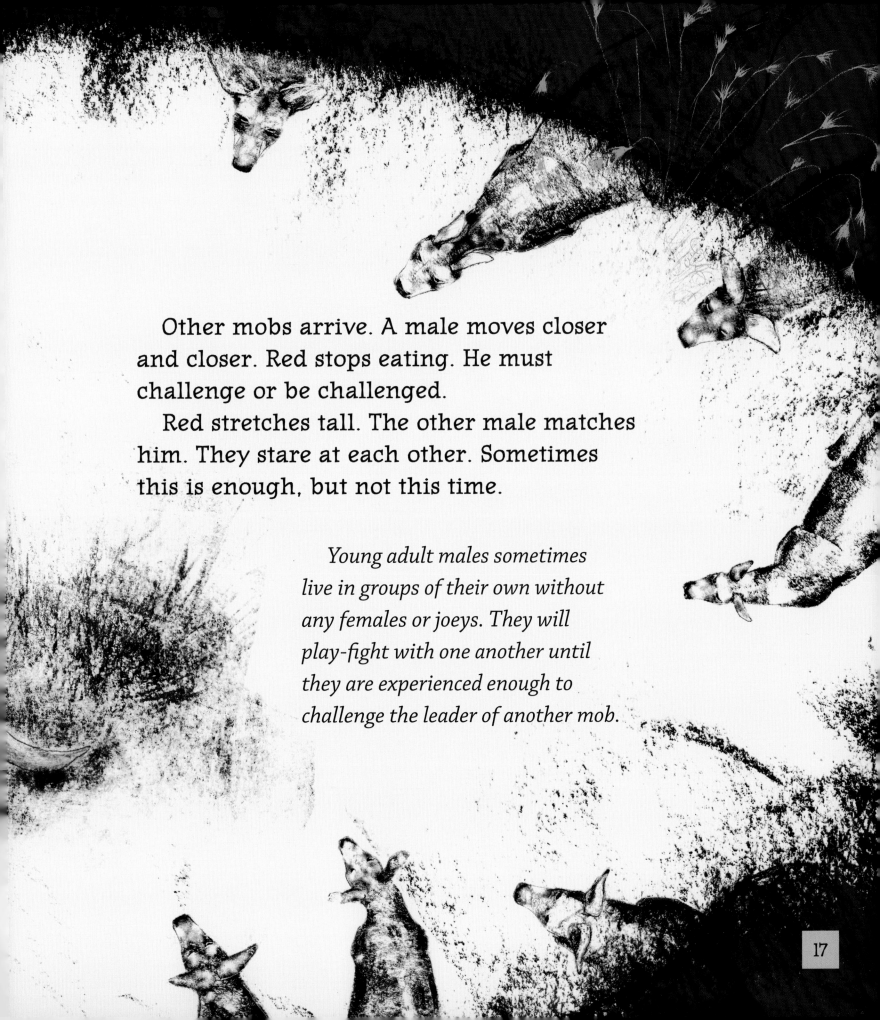

Other mobs arrive. A male moves closer
and closer. Red stops eating. He must
challenge or be challenged.

Red stretches tall. The other male matches
him. They stare at each other. Sometimes
this is enough, but not this time.

Young adult males sometimes
live in groups of their own without
any females or joeys. They will
play-fight with one another until
they are experienced enough to
challenge the leader of another mob.

17

Red pushes up on his toes, bracing against his tail. He tips his head back and lashes out—first one paw, then the other. The other male strikes too, but wildly. Red's next hit will end it.

The challenger retreats, all fight gone from him.

Fights for dominance can be fierce but are usually brief. The loser will withdraw before either kangaroo is really hurt.

Red traverses the open plains with his mob.

As the sun peeks over the horizon, he returns to the trees. They will offer shade and shelter during the sizzle-bright day.

His belly is full.

His mob is safe.

Red is king of his world. For now.

When a male kangaroo is no longer the biggest or strongest, his mob will follow a new leader. This gives the mob the best chance of survival in a harsh environment.

INFORMATION ABOUT RED KANGAROOS

Kangaroos are found only in Australia and Papua New Guinea. They are a diverse family, with more than sixty different species, and live in a wide range of habitats, from wet rainforests to dry plains.

Kangaroos are marsupials—their young are born undeveloped and then continue to grow in their mothers' pouches.

Their family name, *macropod*, means "big foot." The biggest of all macropods is the red kangaroo. They live in the hot, dry inland of Australia, where food can be scarce and water even more so.

INDEX

chewing 5, 14

dawn 5

digestion 5

dingoes.............................14, 15

dusk......................................5

ears......................................2

energy 13

females..............................2, 3

fighting............................17, 19

food 5, 11, 23

goannas.................................15

grass.....................................5

hopping.......................8, 12, 13

joeys 2, 3, 15

licking 1

males 3, 8, 9, 12, 17, 19, 21

mobs.................2, 3, 5, 6, 8, 9,
                      10, 12, 17, 20, 21

rain......................................10

regurgitation 5

shelter 8, 20

spinifex 11

spinifex hopping mouse......10

sun.................................1, 20

survival 21

tails...............................6, 7, 19

thorny devils...................10, 11

wallaroos........................10, 11

water 10, 11, 23

Look up the pages to find out all about kangaroo things.

Don't forget to look at both kinds of words—

this kind and *this kind*.